DINOSAURS
and the Bible

by David Unfred

DINOSAURS AND THE BIBLE

Huntington House Publishers
P.O. Box 53788
Lafayette, LA 70505

For information contact Huntington House Publishers

ISBN 0-910311-70-6

Printed at R.R. Donnelley/USA

Library of Congress Card Number 90-80887

Printed in Colombia.
Impreso en Colombia.

$\mathbb{C}$ ontents

Chapter One

Did Dinosaurs Really Exist?

DOES THE BIBLE TELL US ABOUT DINOSAURS?

ONE OF THE OLDEST books in the Bible is the book of Job. This book was written soon after the great worldwide Flood of Noah's time. Job tells us some fascinating things about this forgotten world—about cave people, about great amounts of ice that could have covered the oceans, and even about snow in places that are now deserts! In Chapter 40, God talks with Job about a special creature He made. Can you discover the identity of this mystery animal, called "behemoth"? Follow the clues to find out!

Clue One: In his mouth were large, long teeth, but he ate grass like the cow and ox. The mountain plants, meadows, trees, and shrubs provided him food.

Clue Four: He enjoyed resting in the water shaded by the willow tree. He was so mighty that even if the largest river flooded, he was not scared.

Clue Five: No one could trap him, even when he was not looking.

Clue Two: He was gentle. Other animals of the forest and fields would play beside him.

Clue Three: He was strong. His back legs were his strength and his belly was the source of his power. His bones were like tubes of brass and like bars of iron.

Clue Seven: He was a giant, the greatest of all the land beasts that God had made.

Clue Six: His tail was like the trunk of a large tree, but could bend like a branch in the wind.

Many creation scientists (men and women who believe that the Bible is a true story about the past) also believe that God was talking to Job about one of the great dinosaurs. If this is the first description of a dinosaur, then we also know something that no scientist will ever know about dinosaurs by studying their fossil bones—God has told us what this dinosaur ate and how he behaved.

Here is an important lesson: There is only one way that we can know anything for sure about the "prehistoric" past—from an eyewitness account! Someone who was there has to tell us what happened. The best eyewitness is someone who is fully knowledgeable and truthful.

God, Himself, is our best eyewitness. He is the Creator who made everything. He is omniscient—the One who knows everything that has happened, will happen, and could possibly happen. God has told us that His Bible is true. It is intended to teach us, to correct us, and to train us in His righteousness (II Timothy 3:16). When the Bible tells us about what happened long ago, it is truthful, just as when we are told about angels, Heaven, Hell, and other things that we cannot see.

When the Bible tells us about the beginning of the world, or about the worldwide Flood, it is God speaking to us; He is teaching us. If we know what happened in the past, then we can better understand the world around us—and more importantly, our relationship to God.

When God tells us through His Bible that He created the heavens and the Earth, the sea, and ALL that is in them in only six days, we can believe Him (Exodus 20:11). This also means that God made all of the giant reptiles that lived on the Earth, in the seas, and even those that flew in the air.

At the time of the great worldwide Flood, God told us that He saved at least two of ALL kinds of air-breathing land animals on the Ark (Genesis 7:15). Does this mean that dinosaurs were on Noah's Ark? Yes, at least one pair of each kind of dinosaur was on the Ark—God said so, and He cannot lie.

If God cannot lie, then why is there still confusion today about dinosaurs and the Bible? God made the dinosaurs and God saved the dinosaurs on Noah's Ark. His Bible tells us so. The problem comes when we believe the ideas of people, who are often wrong and make mistakes, rather than believe the Words of God that are always right!

WHAT CAN SCIENCE TELL US ABOUT DINOSAURS?

We can see pictures of dinosaurs every-where, from stories on television and movie screens, to cereal boxes and even candy wrappers!

Dinosaurs are studied in schools around the world, and hundreds of books have been written about these ancient reptiles. But are all of these ideas about dinosaurs true? What does science tell us about dinosaurs?

Many fossils of dead plants and animals, including dinosaur bones and footprints, are found in rocks all over the world. These rocks are called "sedimentary rocks." Most sedimentary rocks were made when thick layers of mud, stirred up by great amounts of water, became hard (similar to the way wet concrete in a building or sidewalk becomes rock solid). Creation scientists believe that fossils in most sedimentary rocks are from animals killed and buried during Noah's Flood.

Chemicals in the mud have changed millions of animal shells and bones into stone. Over time, sedimentary rocks hiding these fossils have been worn down by wind and water, sometimes breaking off to show the fossil remains of animals and plants that died so very suddenly—but *not* so long ago.

Since the Great Flood, people have found huge fossil bones and fossil footprints of animals in rocks. People thought that these bones and footprints belonged to giant animals, perhaps even monsters. Maybe they had heard stories about the giant reptiles that God had saved on Noah's Ark. Could this be why stories of dragons are told all over the world, from ancient times to now?

WHO DISCOVERED DINOSAURS?

The first known dinosaur fossil bones were found by Dr. Mantell, a medical doctor, and his wife Mary Anne. Both enjoyed collecting fossils. One day in 1822, Mary Anne found a rock with a fossil tooth buried in it. The rock would not have been special to many people; "It's just like all the rest," they would have said. Other people, like Mary Anne, would discover hidden and sometimes strange secrets in otherwise ordinary stones. You could, too!

Mary Anne hurried to find her husband and share her discovery. Soon she and Dr. Mantell had uncovered a whole collection of teeth and even some fossil bones, but they had no idea what kind of animal the fossils could have belonged to. Finally, the Mantells sent their discovery to Paris to one of the greatest scientists they knew, Baron Georges Cuvier.

Baron Cuvier was a founder of the science of paleontology—the study of fossil animals. The Baron believed that many of the fossils being discovered (like those found by the Mantells) were those of animals suddenly buried during a terrible flood—the Great Flood of the Bible.

When Baron Cuvier opened the package, we can only imagine what he must have thought. The fossils were strange, unlike any animal with which he was familiar. He could have compared the fossils to his own collection of teeth from living animals, or possibly his collection of tooth drawings.

He identified the teeth as possibly being from a kind of rhinoceros that was extinct (no longer living), and he thought the fossil bones might have belonged to an extinct hippopotamus. Dr. Mantell, however, was not convinced with this answer.

Three years later, Dr. Mantell met a man who studied iguana lizards of Mexico and Central America. Dr. Mantell showed the scientist his collection of fossil teeth. The teeth looked very much like iguana teeth, only much larger. With this new information, Dr. Mantell named his "fossil iguana," *Iguanodon* (ig-WAN-o-don). Later, when Baron Cuvier heard of Dr.

Mantell's discovery, like the great scientist he was, Cuvier admitted his error and predicted that a whole new group of fossil animals would be discovered.

A few years later, one of England's most honored scientists, William Buckland, added to the idea of giant fossil lizards. Professor Buckland taught and did research at Oxford University. His training was in the science of geology, the study of the Earth. He was a Christian who believed the Bible was truly God's Word. As a creationist, he wrote a number of books showing the evidence of God's design in minerals and rocks. While at Oxford, Professor Buckland was given some strange fossil bones. After careful study, he concluded that the bones belonged to a big meat-eating reptile, which he named *Megalosaurus* (meg-a-lo-SORE-us) or "giant lizard."

HOW DINOSAURS GOT THEIR NAME

As Baron Georges Cuvier predicted, many fossil "lizard" bones continued to be discovered. Twenty years after the Mantells' discovery of *Iguanodon* teeth, Sir Richard Owen, the famous British scientist, suggested a name for all of the fossil reptiles—that name was *Dinosauria,* from which we get "dinosaur" or "terrible lizard." As superintendent of the Natural History Department of the British Museum, Sir Richard Owen used the fossil bones to build dinosaur models. Some of these early models are shown on the next page.

Sir Richard Owen believed in God. He also believed that God created the world and every living thing in it. But his belief was not shared by all scientists. Many of the scientists living before him had believed that life could arise suddenly from dead things. This idea was called "spontaneous generation." These scientists observed that flies and other small animals seemed to come from rotting meat or moldy hay. They did not believe the Bible, which states that all living things give birth to their own kind: Potato bugs make more potato bugs, and dogs make more dogs, but spoiled hamburgers do not make flies—flies make more flies!

During Sir Richard Owen's lifetime, another idea about how life began became popular. Simply told, one man, Charles Darwin, convinced many people that new kinds of animals could come from different kinds of animals through accidental changes, called variations. Darwin believed the offspring of these "changed" animals

Early reconstructions of dinosaur models relied more on imagination than the study of living reptiles. Scientists today still rely on imagination to guess at dinosaur coloration, skin form, and behavior. Until a living dinosaur is found, a scientist can only study dead fossils buried in rocks that were formed from mud laid down by catastrophic flooding.

Mammals such as whales, dolphins, and manatees are difficult to explain by evolution. Some evolutionists believe that four-legged land animals, similar to water buffalos or hippopotumi, stayed in water so long that they "evolved" into animals that could only exist in the ocean habitat. In reality, no biological mechanism exists to suggest the possibility of this or any other process of "evolution."

would have been different. He also guessed that over very, very long periods of time, some of the changed animals were better able to survive. According to Darwin's idea, they were supposed to be stronger, better able to find food, and better able to adjust to changes in the weather. This idea is called evolution.

Darwin's "new" idea about how life began convinced many people who chose not to believe in creation, but not Sir Richard Owen. In fact, Professor Owen became a strong warrior against evolution. His vast knowledge of fossils told him that there was no evidence for one kind of animal changing into another kind—and he would still be correct today. Almost 150 years later, no fossil evidence for evolution has ever been found.

It may sound as odd as dead meat changing into flies, but scientists who believe in evolution think that given enough time, cows could have changed into whales. Given even more time, they believe, hydrogen gas became people! Such an idea is incredible to anyone with common sense, yet many scientists still believe in Darwin's idea. Why? Because they accept evolution by faith, not by scientific evidence. The Bible book of Romans, 1:20-25, describes scientists and people who have *chosen* not to believe in a Creator, in spite of overwhelming evidence.

True science, based on observation, logic, and knowledge, will always support what the Bible teaches.

WHAT DAY WERE THE DINOSAURS MADE?

God tells us in the Bible that He made the universe and every living thing in six days. God could do this because He is omnipotent, meaning all-powerful. His power is not limited. God made all of nature from nothing. He could have made the world in six seconds or six billion years, but He didn't. He took six days. God tells us why He took this long in the Bible book of Exodus 20:8-11. God is speaking directly to Moses on Mount Sinai:

Remember the Sabbath day, to keep it holy. Six days you will labor and do all your work, but the seventh day is the Sabbath of the Lord your God. In it you will do no work—you, nor your son, nor your daughter, nor your male servant, nor your female servant, nor your cattle, nor your stranger who is within your gates. For in six days the Lord made the heavens and the earth, the sea, and all that is in them, and rested the seventh day. Therefore the Lord blessed the Sabbath day and hallowed it.

Today few people remember how the idea of a seven day week began, or even that one day is to be set aside to worship our Creator. By reading the Bible,

CREATION WEEK

we find that from the very beginning, one week has always been seven days. It was during this first week that God made the dinosaurs.

The Bible book of Genesis is the book of beginnings, where God tells us what He did on each day of the Creation week. But when did He create the dinosaurs?

On the sixth day, God made animals that could be tamed to serve people—cattle, sheep, camels, and horses. He also created the wild beasts—like mammoths, saber-toothed cats, moles, and many other "creeping things." All of the land animals were made on this day, including every kind of dinosaur that lived on land.

Chapter Two

Destruction of the Dinosaurs

H UMAN BEINGS and all animals were created to be vegetarians, or plant eaters. All animals would have continued to eat plants except for one terrible thing: Our great, great, many-great grand-parents, Adam and Eve (the first man and woman God created) rebelled against His perfect plan for their lives. When this happened, death came into the world for the first time. The first murder happened when Adam and Eve's son, Cain, killed his younger brother.

By looking at the fossil record, we can find evidence that death and violence also came to the rest of creation. All of creation suffered because of man's disobedience to God. Things became so bad that God destroyed all life—all except for the people and animals on Noah's Ark.

THE TIME OF THE GREAT FLOOD

All animals living today have ancestors found as fossils. There are also animals found as fossils that are no longer living. Many different ideas are given for this great "mass extinction." What caused the death of so many animals, including the dinosaurs?

Violence in the pre-Flood world is often captured in the fossil record. This particular fossil also demonstrates rapid burial and fossilization.

Dapalis Macrurus: Courtesy of Ron Calais

Today we find huge fossil graveyards containing the jumbled bones of many different animals. In some parts of the world, thousands of dinosaurs have been destroyed and buried together. Were they killed while crossing a flooded river, as one scientist suggests? Some fossils are in sedimentary rocks containing volcanic ash. Were dinosaurs killed by a sudden explosion of volcanoes all over the Earth? Not long ago, scientists discovered evidence that sedimentary rocks contain traces of asteroids, buried along with fossil bones and shells. Were dinosaurs killed when a giant asteroid hit the earth? Or maybe the weather changed. Did the dinosaurs starve to death when their food was destroyed by the ice and cold weather of the Ice Age? Do any one of these explanations fit all of the evidence, or is the best answer one that would combine several ideas? Could the reason for the death of so many animals and plants be the Flood of Noah's time? Let's look at the evidence and see if we can find the answer.

Here is a fact: Billions and billions of dead things have been buried in mud, which eventually turned into rock. When we look at the Grand Canyon, we see layer upon layer of this mud, thousands of feet deep, turned to rock. It is easy to see these layers in the Grand Canyon, but did you know that sedimentary rocks cover 75 percent of the Earth's land surface? What mighty force could lay down thousands of feet of mud, all over the Earth? Again, we find the best answer in God's Bible: The Great Flood.

Many people have heard of the Flood, but it would be very hard for any of us to imagine how terrible the great destruction really was. Have you been in a bad earthquake? Have you seen what can happen when a volcano explodes? Have you been near a killer tornado or hurricane? Nothing that you may have seen or heard about is even close to what happened during the first few minutes of the Flood!

To get an idea of how frightening and terrible the Flood could have been, we can look at catastrophes that have happened not so long ago and what people wrote about them. All of these terrible things happened in just one small part of the world—as you read these reports, imagine if they happened all over the Earth at the same time.

Many different strata of sedimentary rock are observed along the walls of the Grand Canyon in Arizona. These strata show evidence of having been soft mud when deposited and when the canyon was formed.

WHAT HAPPENS WHEN A VOLCANO EXPLODES?

On August 27, 1883, the island volcano, Krakatoa (Crack ah TOE ah), exploded. More than 36,000 people lost their lives. An English sea captain was sailing many miles away from the island when the volcano erupted and kept a record of what he saw. Here is what he wrote in his ship's log:

The blinding fall of sand and stones, the intense blackness above and around us, broken only by the unceasing glare of various kinds of lightning and the continuous explosive roar of Krakatoa, made our situation a truly awful one. (Near midnight) the island, eleven miles away, became more visible. Chains of fire appeared to rise and fall between the sky, while in the southwest we could see a continuous roll of balls of white fire. The strong wind (that blew across the ship) was hot and choking, and smelled like sulfur and burning cinders. Parts of the ship glowed with electricity...

These horrible things continued into the next day, but the most frightening catastrophe was still to come. Under the ship rolled two giant waves traveling at a great speed. As they reached the shores of the islands around Krakatoa, the waves rose higher and higher. When the towering killer waves slammed onto the islands, all of the villages, animals, and people vanished. It was as if they had never existed. Tsunami (soo NAH me) is the name given to these giant killer waves.

About the time that Moses was leading the children of Israel out of Egypt, the island volcano of Thera exploded in the Mediterranean Sea. Scientists have calculated that the tsunami that hit the neighboring island of Crete was traveling at 200 miles an hour. When it crashed over the island, the wave would have been 300 feet high!

In 1815, the island volcano of Tambora in Indonesia exploded. Great amounts of dust were thrown high into the sky. A year later, dust from the volcano was still being carried by wind currents at great heights. Like a mirror, the dust reflected warm sunlight back into space. In the northern parts of the world that summer, it was very cold. Some newspapers called 1816 "the year without a summer." During that summer, snow fell in New England in June, and crop-killing frosts continued through August! In Europe, thousands of people starved from the resulting famine.

These stories are historical accounts of what just one volcano can do to the world around it. Imagine what would have happened when thousands of volcanoes, very much like Krakatoa, Thera, and Tambora, exploded at the same time all over the earth!

WHAT HAPPENS DURING AN EARTHQUAKE?

During 1811 and 1812, the Mississippi River Valley was violently shaken by earthquakes centered around New Madrid, Missouri. These earthquakes were more powerful than the more famous California earthquakes and were felt more than 1,000 miles away. Some of the people living in New Madrid described what they saw and felt during one earthquake on February 7, 1812:

> **The ground shook violently. Giant cracks (called fissures) ran suddenly over the ground like the branches of a tree. Some of the cracks were thirty feet wide and 700 feet long. Water, sand, and something like coal, spouted out of the cracks as high as forty feet into the air!**
> **Some of the cracks would break open, then close up again just as quickly. The sky was awfully dark and the air smelled of sulfur. Thunder and light flashed from explosions within the cracks, and together with lightning shooting from cloud to cloud, brightened the sky while the earth shook.**
> **The Mississippi River seemed to dry up, leaving boats high on dry land, but suddenly the river water returned in a wall fifteen to twenty feet high, destroying all of the boats along the river banks, drowning forests, and creating new lakes.**

Areas of the town of New Madrid were fifteen feet lower after the earthquake stopped. If an earthquake this powerful happened today, hundreds of thousands of people would perish.

Imagine what would have happened during the time of the Flood when thousands of earthquakes, a hundred thousand times more powerful than the one in New Madrid, began at the same time all over the Earth.

WHAT HAPPENS WHEN ASTEROIDS AND COMETS HIT THE EARTH?

Have you ever wondered why the Moon has thousands of craters, formed by asteroid hits? All of Earth's neighboring planets (Mercury, Venus, and Mars) also have cratered surfaces. It looks like a huge rock shower blasted these planets—but if so, then why does Earth show so little evidence of being hit? Could the evidence of asteroid craters on Earth have been erased somehow, perhaps by the powerful waters of a worldwide flood?

The Bible tells us that at the beginning of the Great Flood, the "windows of heaven" were opened, and the "waters," held above the Earth's atmosphere, rained down for forty days and nights. Could comets and asteroids have been part of the "waters above"?

A comet is like a huge, dirty snowball, made of rock and ice. As it travels toward the Sun, the Sun's heat begins to change the surface of the comet to gas. These gases, and small pieces of dust and ice, form a comet "tail" that always points away from the Sun.

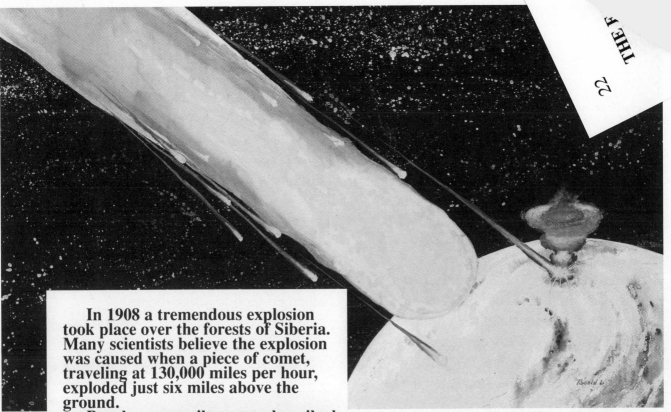

In 1908 a tremendous explosion took place over the forests of Siberia. Many scientists believe the explosion was caused when a piece of comet, traveling at 130,000 miles per hour, exploded just six miles above the ground.

People many miles away described a huge black cloud that appeared immediately after the explosion. A heat wave burned trees for twelve miles around the center of the explosion, followed by a shock wave through the air. The force of this shock wave knocked down eighty million trees over many miles of forest, and killed thousands of reindeer.

The dust of the comet's tail, as it continued to travel beyond Earth and away from the Sun, caused the night sky over Western Russia and Europe to be unusually bright.

Scientists have calculated what would happen if one comet, just six miles in diameter, were to hit the Earth. The explosion would cause ocean waves, more than 1,000 feet high, to run for at least 600 miles from where the comet splashed into the water. When this tsunami approached land, it would become a wave thousands of feet high and travel for hundreds of miles across land.

Currents of hot, liquid rock deep within the center of the Earth would be disturbed, causing changes in the Earth's magnetic field. Deep cracks would form in the Earth's outer crust. Mountains would rise up rapidly, volcanoes would explode all over the Earth, and massive areas of land would be covered by molten lava. Ozone, an important gas high in the atmosphere that protects us from harmful ultraviolet sunlight, would be destroyed. All around the world, powerful earthquakes would shake both land and sea. No one living today has seen such a catastrophe.

Look at the Moon through binoculars or a telescope tonight and study its cratered surface. Imagine what would happen if hundreds of asteroids and comets hit the Earth at the same time, and you will have part of an idea of the complete destruction of the Earth during Noah's Flood.

EIGHTH DAY

Even though we know of terrible destructions like the ones you have read here, we can only imagine how terrible the power of the Great Flood must have been. Why did God destroy the Earth in such a terrible way? The Bible tells us the reason.

Because people enjoyed disobeying God, violence filled the Earth. If God had not destroyed the world, the small, faithful family of Noah's would have been destroyed by the evil of the world in which they lived. But because of God's love, He had Noah tell the people of the coming judgment for 120 years. Were the people worried? No, they only laughed and went about their lives as usual, unconcerned with the things of God.

What were the thoughts of these doomed people as God brought the animals into the Ark? Did they become concerned when God sealed the Ark shut? Again, we can only imagine, but we know that for seven days, Noah, his family, and the animals were sealed in the Ark—and nothing happened. Were Noah and his family a big joke among the people, who were enjoying bright sunny days outside the Ark?

On the eighth day, the Flood began. We can imagine how water rained down from above, as never before. The ground shook from thousands of mighty earthquakes, and the waters trapped beneath the Earth exploded out of the ground. Great walls of water, steam, and choking gases shot high into the sky. Volcanic explosions filled the air with black clouds of ash and rock. Darkness fell over the whole Earth.

Before the Flood was finished, large basins to hold the world's oceans were formed. Flood waters rushed off the land, forming great canyons and rock formations. Mountains rose up where there had been no mountains before. Thousands of feet of mud, containing billions of dead plants and animals, hardened into vaults of rock, storing billions of fossils as reminders of the terrible judgment.

The "eighth day" began the year-long destruction of a world that had turned away from God's love—a world that had challenged God to judge them.

A GRAVEYARD FOR REMEMBERING

One valley in France, where coal mining is important, is a graveyard of plants and animals. It contains the fossils of ocean animals, freshwater amphibians, and land animals such as spiders, scorpions, millipedes, and reptiles. All these animals were suddenly buried together, entombed in the same rock. It is fossil graveyards like these, all over the world, that remind us of the terrible and sudden destruction of the Great Flood of the Bible.

Chapter Three

Dinosaur Mysteries and the Bible

A LOT OF GUESSING surrounds questions about the dinosaurs. Science can only study what happens in the present and guess about what might have happened long ago, but the Bible is God's true record of what happened in the past. Can the Bible, as a record from the very beginning, help solve some of these dinosaur mysteries?

MYSTERY: WHAT HAPPENED TO THE DINOSAURS?

Evidence of sudden death can be found all over the Earth, in massive fossil graveyards. Where did all of these animals come from, and how were they buried? After looking at some of these "graveyards," it's not hard to see that the biblical record of the Great Flood explains the death of the dinosaurs. One fossil hunter found a rock "tomb" containing a herd of almost 10,000 dinosaur skeletons. The Flood also explains the death of the many other animals whose fossils are found in the layers of rock (called the "fossil record").

What killed the dinosaurs? For those who don't believe the Bible, the popular theory is that a large asteroid hit the Earth, killing the great reptiles and other life at that time. As we have seen, such an asteroid strike could cause volcanoes to explode over the Earth, create huge ocean waves that rush over land, and throw dust into our atmosphere, creating unusual changes in temperature.

This is important! People who don't believe the Bible are getting closer and closer to what the Bible teaches about the Flood. Why? Because, as scientists study evidence in the world around us, it becomes harder to reject true history, which is recorded in God's Word.

Job tells of ice-covered oceans and frozen rivers (Job 37:9-10).

In the time just after the Flood, there were not as many plants. This made it difficult for extremely large animals to survive on a new diet and less food. As the world got colder, and large glaciers covered the northern lands, even the wooly mammoth and wooly rhinoceros perished. It may not be surprising, then, that today, the largest land animals live naturally in the warmer parts of the world.

After the Flood, people could also have hunted dinosaurs. Legends of people who killed dragons are found in every ancient civilization. We can imagine that people might have feared the strange reptiles and wanted their destruction.

Even today, elephants and rhinoceros (as well as many other animals) are now in danger of becoming extinct. People have hunted the huge animals for their ivory tusks and horns. Humans have also changed the environment, creating desert where grassland and forest used to be. It will take courageous, godly men and women, boys and girls, to find the correct balance for taking care of God's creation as well as the needs of people.

But what happened to the dinosaurs on Noah's Ark? If God really did put at least two of every kind of animal on the Ark, why aren't dinosaurs still living? The world after the Flood was very different. It was cooler, and for a time, probably much colder than it is today. In the Bible, the ancient book of

MYSTERY: WHY WERE SOME DINOSAURS SO LARGE?

Dinosaurs came in all sizes. The smallest dinosaur is believed to be *Compsognathus* (comp-so-NATH-us), which was the size of a chicken. The largest dinosaur fossils are called the sauropods. One of the largest is the *Brachiosaurus* (broc-ee-o-SORE-us). A fossil skeleton of a *Brachiosaurus* in the Museum of Natural History in Berlin, Germany, is forty-two feet tall. But even this dinosaur skeleton is not the largest.

Sauropod fossils found in the western United States have been given the name "Ultrasaurus" because of their huge size. These giants were more than ninety-eight feet long and sixty feet tall—as high as a six-story building! The longest dinosaur known is the "Seismosaurus," or "earth-shaker." Its fossil skeleton was found in New Mexico. When alive, this dinosaur may have been 140 feet long and weighed fifty tons. This "terrible lizard" was so large that two seismosaurs standing nose to nose would cover a football field!

Some dinosaurs hatched from eggs. What size egg would it take to make one of these giants? Well, the largest known fossil egg doesn't belong to a dinosaur at all. The egg of the extinct "elephant bird" from Madagascar could hold almost 8.9 liters, or 2.35 gallons, of water. The largest fossil dinosaur egg is about ten inches long and could hold about 3.3 liters, or less than one gallon.

A hill in western Montana, named Egg Mountain, contains nests of fossil *Maiasaura* (me-a-SORE-ah) eggs. This discovery was important because some nests also had fossils of young dinosaurs. The adult dinosaur grew to be about thirty feet long, but the pear-shaped eggs were only about two inches wide and seven inches long. Here is the mystery: How does an animal so large grow from an egg so small?

Fossil dinosaur egg nest in Argentina.

We know that many living reptiles grow throughout their lives. Is it possible that some dinosaurs lived to be much older than reptiles today? If they did live longer, they could have grown much, much larger—even to the size of the giants that we find in the fossil graveyards. In the book of Genesis we are told that people before the Flood lived to be as much as 900 years old. What would happen if dinosaurs also lived more than twelve times longer than modern reptiles?

Could the giant "earth-shaker" seismosaurus have been a several-hundred-year-old sauropod?

Science can be used to guess the size of a dinosaur from its fossils, but can science guess how long the animal lived? Thin slices of some dinosaur bones, when examined under a microscope, show a structure called a "Haversian canal." It is rare for living reptiles to have many of these canals. But very large, very old crocodiles are known to have a few scattered canals.

This discovery suggests that the longer a reptile lives, more canals will form inside its bones. In some dinosaur fossils, an enormously large number of canals are found. Could this be evidence of a reptile that lived a very long time—perhaps to be several hundred years old?

MYSTERY: COULD DINOSAURS HAVE LIVED NEAR THE NORTH POLE?

Dinosaur fossils have been found in ice-cold regions as far north as Canada and Alaska. How could these dinosaurs have survived in the cold, and what did they eat, especially when the snow fell? This is a mystery.

Creation scientists believe that before the Flood, the Earth was a very pleasant place to live. Tropical and subtropical fruit trees have been found in parts of the world that are now permanently frozen. Other fossil plants and animals suggest that at one time Earth was warm all over.

Some creation scientists believe that before the Flood, a canopy of water vapor surrounded the Earth (Genesis 1:6-7). Such a canopy could have caused a mild "greenhouse effect." (The greenhouse effect refers to a condition when more of the Sun's warmth is trapped in the Earth's atmosphere; less heat escapes back into space.) In this type of greenhouse environment, dinosaurs, other animals, and even man would have lived just as comfortably at the north and south polar regions of the Earth as anywhere else on the planet.

After the Flood, however, ice and snow began to fall on the northern and southern poles. Just because dinosaur fossils are found in rocks buried under ice and snow, does that mean the animals lived in the cold? No, especially since there is evidence that other warmth-loving plants and animals died at the same time, in the same place. Again, the history of the world recorded in the Bible can help us solve the "Mystery of the Polar Dinosaurs."

MYSTERY: HOW DID DINOSAUR TRACKS TURN INTO ROCK?

Dinosaur tracks can tell us certain things about the animal that made them—for example, how fast the dinosaur moved and how heavy it was. Places where many fossil dinosaur tracks are found together suggest that when in danger, some plant-eating dinosaur herds surrounded their young to protect them (from a great wall of water?) Dinosaur tracks also tell us that these great reptiles lived all over the world at the time of the Flood.

Tyrannosaurus (ty-ran-no-SORE-us) tracks suggest that it could run forty-five miles per hour—that's sixty-six feet per second. No human, not even an Olympic athlete, could have outrun a living *Tyrannosaurus*—especially if it was running from a rushing wall of water!

The big mystery is how dinosaur tracks turned into rock. Everyone leaves tracks when they walk through mud. If more rain does not wash them away, the mud-tracks dry out and become hard, but they do not turn into rock. Wind, or the next rainstorm, will make them disappear. Why, then, have some dinosaur tracks turned to rock?

Perhaps this wasn't ordinary mud over which the dinosaur walked (or ran). In fact, this is true. The mud churned up and laid down by the Flood contained many special minerals. As the mud began to dry, these chemicals helped to harden the mud into rock—much the same way that concrete hardens. Sometimes animals and people

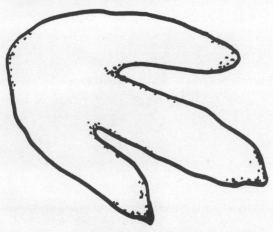

accidently walk on wet cement leaving paw prints or footprints—just as dinosaurs moving across the soft Flood mud left their tracks. The mud hardened, making a fossil record of the dinosaurs' tracks. Then, more mud covered the tracks, saving them for future discovery. Like fossil bones saved in stone, fossil dinosaur tracks remind us of the terrible results of God's judgement.

MYSTERY TRACKS IN TEXAS

For many years, people have described what they believed to be human footprints along with dinosaur footprints in the Paluxy riverbed rock, near Glen Rose, Texas. The Bible tells us that all living things were created in one week; therefore, people and dinosaurs lived at the same time. The Bible also tells us that God placed at least two of every kind of creature on Noah's Ark. Is there evidence of dinosaurs and people together at the Paluxy? Evolutionists do not want any evidence to exist for man and dinosaurs living at the same time. Creationists would not be surprised at all, though, if evidence of people and dinosaurs were found together. After looking at this photograph of a recent dinosaur trail excavation, what do you think?

Fossil animal tracks, particularly dinosaurs', occur in the Paluxy River sediments near Glen Rose, Texas. Several "trails" of human-like footprints are found crossing dinosaurs tracks. One famous trail has what appears to be a human footprint within and alongside a three-toed dinosaur track.

MYSTERY: COULD GIANT REPTILES FLY?

The *Pterosaurs* (ter-o-SORES) are not really dinosaurs, but "winged reptiles." The smallest pterosaur fossils are no larger than a sparrow. The largest pterosaur is *Quetzalcoatlus* (KET sawl co AT luss). This giant's wingspan was fifty feet—that's larger than a modern jet fighter! This reptile was huge, all right, but could *Quetzalcoatlus* fly?

Pterosaurs had large bodies and narrow wings. Many scientists cannot imagine how this animal could have flown. Some have suggested that pterosaurs had to climb to the tops of cliffs or into the tops of trees and would glide—much like a flying squirrel would. Can you imagine *Quetzalcoatlus* gliding off a hundred-foot high cliff and then having to hike back to the top to jump again?

Fortunately for the "Big 'Q'," pterosaur fossil bones show that they had strong flight muscles. Early creation scientists, like Baron Cuvier and Sir Richard Owen, thought that pterosaurs were able to fly, but only now are today's scientists rediscovering that pterosaurs do have the unique skeleton

of a powerful flyer. It makes a lot more sense to believe that *Quetzalcoatlus* used its strong muscles and giant wingspan to fly, and not to crawl.

Creation scientists may have additional evidence to support the flight theory. If a canopy of water surrounded the Earth before the Flood, then the air below the canopy would have been denser, or

"thicker," than it is today. And if the air was denser, it would have been easier for the large pterosaurs to fly. There are several other benefits of this "dense air" theory. For one, the high pressure of the air would have made it easier for the giant reptiles, like the seismosaurs, to breathe. These animals would have otherwise found it very difficult to get enough oxygen to supply their huge bodies.

Chapter Four

Are Dinosaurs Still Living?

MANY SCIENTISTS, as well as Bible teachers, believe that the Flood of the Bible happened a little more than 4,000 years ago. Scripture tells us that God saved representatives of every kind of air-breathing animal from the Flood's destruction. Since dinosaur kinds were on Noah's Ark, then perhaps some are still living today. Other people believe that dinosaurs lived and became extinct millions of years before humans walked on Earth. Is there more evidence that dinosaurs and people have lived at the same time? Let's look at some evidence from cryptozoology (KRIP toe zoe OL o jee)—the scientific search for "hidden animals." As scientists have searched the hard to reach areas on land and in the oceans, some startling discoveries have been made.

THE FISH THAT GOT AWAY

How can you know how old a fossil is? The answer is that no one can know any fossil's true age for sure. Many methods that scientists use to guess the ages of fossils are built on guesses themselves. For example, one method uses a system based on "index fossils." One famous index fossil was the *coelacanth* (SEE luh kanth), a fossil fish. Scientists were sure at one time that the coelacanth became extinct sixty million years ago. Any rocks, therefore, that had coelacanth fossils in them, were assumed to be sixty million years old—in fact, all fossils found in those rocks were believed to be that old too.

Using this "index fossil" system, we could go on and on thinking in circles, but would we be even closer in guessing the true age of either the coelacanth fossil or the rock in which it was buried?

One evening in 1938, a fishing trawler arrived at its dock, having just brought a catch in from the ocean. As the fishermen sorted through their catch, they discovered a fish they had never seen before. It was nearly six feet long, with powerful jaws, strong lobe-shaped fins, and heavy rough scales. Its color was steel blue with scattered pink blotches. News of this strange fish spread quickly through the town. Finally, the dead fish (that was also beginning to smell like a dead fish), arrived at the laboratory of a university chemist. Immediately, he recognized it. Without a doubt, it was a coelacanth!

Today other living coelacanths have been found and studied. Photographs have even been taken of them at home on the ocean floor. Before the discovery of this fish, most scientists believed coelacanths and people did not live at the same time. Surprise! Coelacanths and people have always lived together, and they still do. Here is a question to think about: How old is a coelacanth fossil and the rock in which the fossil is buried?

THE LAST PTEROSAUR?

From time to time, people have reported seeing living pterosaurs (ter-o-SORES). Like the coelacanth, according to evolutionists, pterosaurs are supposed to have all died sixty-five million years ago.

In 1856, workmen digging a railway tunnel in France were using gunpowder to remove a boulder. When the dust settled, the surprised workmen brought a huge bat-like creature out of the tunnel. But the animal wasn't dead. When it reached the light it began to shake its wings, making a hoarse cry. It was shiny black, had a long neck, and rows of sharp teeth in its long beak-like mouth. Soon after it was removed from the mine, it died. Its wingspan was measured to be more than ten feet!

A scientist was called in to examine this strange creature. His conclusion: The animal was a pterosaur.

ARE PLESIOSAURS LIVING IN THE OCEAN?

On April 10, 1977, off the coast of New Zealand, the nets of the Japanese fishing trawler, *Zuiyo Maru*, pulled in an unexpected catch. Filling the net was the rotting body of a recently dead ocean reptile! Not wanting to spoil his other catch, and not realizing the value of his find, the ship's captain had the smelly carcass thrown back into the ocean. But fortunately, they took photographs and measured the monster first.

The animal was thirty-two feet long and weighed approximately 4,000 pounds. The skin had mostly decayed, but in places where it was still attached, it was a pinkish-red color. Tissue samples were saved to be analyzed by the marine scientists when the ship returned to Japan. The best guess was that the mystery animal was a **Plesiosaur** (PLEE zee o sor). A scientist at the famous National Science Museum of Japan said, "It seems that these animals are not extinct after all. It's impossible for only one to have survived. There must be a group."

Although the discovery of a *Plesiosaur* was ignored, excused, and overlooked by European and American scientists, it was called the "scientific discovery of the year" in Japan. So amazing was this find that the Japanese issued a commemorative postage stamp to honor the discovery, shown on the opposite page.

The Search for Mokele-Mbembe

In recent years, scientists from American and Japanese universities have searched the dark jungles of the African Congo. What were they hunting? A living dinosaur the natives call Mokele-Mbembe! (mo-KE-le-MEM-be)

Large animals have been reported for many years in the dangerous Congo swamps and lakes. In one 1980 sighting, a native came to a jungle mission after having seen a strange creature. As his canoe rounded a riverbend, he saw a reddish-brown animal in the water. Above the water was a "snake-like" head, six to eight feet long. As he hurriedly paddled away, more of the animal's back appeared. Later, when looking at artists' pictures of dinosaurs, the native identified the animal as a sauropod, a plant-eating dinosaur!

Another sighting, reported about the

same time, was from a young girl. On her way home along the shore of Lake Tele, her canoe became stuck on a sand bar. Although she tried to dislodge her canoe, something kept pushing her back onto the sand. Suddenly, there was a great amount of splashing, and a large animal broke the water's surface. The terrified girl could not tell the head of the animal from its tail, but she described the body as the size of four elephants. In shock and crying for help, the girl was found by her parents sometime later. When they returned to the place where the mystery animal had been seen, they found prints of a large, unknown animal that they were able to follow for hundreds of feet along the lake shore.

What is important about the stories of the natives and scientists? They are all similar. They also remind us of the description of another animal—the great "behemoth" in the Bible book of Job! Did people and dinosaurs live at the same time? Yes, and they still could!

Chapter Five

What Can Dinosaurs Teach Us?

GOD IS CREATOR

GOD TOLD JOB TO THINK about behemoth. Why? Because by considering this great creature, Job could see the mighty power of God. Job knew that only God could create an animal like the behemoth. For the same reason, our study of dinosaurs today can tell us something about God, our Creator.

God made the universe and everything in it. When we look at His creation, we can know about His power and that He is eternal (Romans 1:18-23). When we study even the smallest part of creation, the amazing design and complexity of many parts working together is hard for us to understand. Could the world and everything in it happen by accident? The correct answer is no. Only

BEFORE THE FLOOD

FLOOD JUDGEMENT

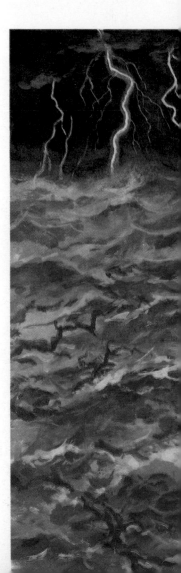

intelligence, an intelligence much greater than our own, can make complex patterns of life with such marvelous design and purpose.

GOD IS JUST

God hates sin. Our first ancestors, Adam and Eve, chose to disobey God. Their action allowed sin into the world. Because God had made Adam responsible for the care, or stewardship, of His Creation, the world and everything in it suffered from the effects of sin (Romans 5:12).

Just like Adam and Eve, we still want to live life without obeying God. Sin still affects creation, and sin is still part of our own nature. But God is just. That means that He must judge sin. The terrible worldwide destruction of the Great Flood shows us how God judges His creation when it turns against Him.

God never changes. He is still Just. Today we live in an evil world, where people are very much like those who lived in Noah's time before the Flood. God promises that sin will not go unpunished.

AFTER THE FLOOD

Even though people may laugh and ask "where is the promise of His coming?" (2 Peter 3:1-10), God is patient. His judgement will destroy the universe and everything in it—not with water, but with fire. Even so, He patiently waits for all who will come to Him.

GOD IS LOVE

God has given Himself to be judged in place of each of us. This mystery is the greatest of all! Jesus, a man without sin, died in our place. So great is God's love for us (John 3:16)!

As in Noah's day, many people are still rejecting God's love. Have you recognized your own sin against God? Have you talked to Him about it? Have you earnestly asked God to forgive you? If not, you can. If you will ask, He will create in you a new life—one that will never die. (Romans 3:10-23; 1 John 1:8-9.) Ask God to save you, to forgive your disobiedence against Him. Ask Him now by praying this simple prayer:

Father God, thank You for creating me and letting me know about You. Thank You for loving me so much that You gave Your Son, Christ Jesus, to be judged for my sin against You. Take my sins against You away and don't count them against me. Thank You for loving me. Thank You for forgiving me. Teach me from Your Bible to be the person You would have me be. Take control of my life from now on so I can do what You would have me do. I will praise You, O Lord, with my whole heart. I will tell others of the marvelous things You have done. I will be glad and will rejoice in You. In the name of Jesus, who made me and saved me, Amen.

APPENDIX A: Tyrannosaurus Rex: The Terrible Melon Eater?

We tend to believe what we see and hear on television and read in books. But true science is not believing what is simply popular. Science is a continuous process of observation and discovery. We also develop hypotheses and models based on scientific facts and our own ideas (biases) about what happened in the past. The following example shows how newly revealed facts can challenge old ideas.

In Genesis, we are told something about dinosaurs that no scientist can know from studying dinosaur fossils:in the beginning, all dinosaurs were plant eaters! In fact, all animals and the first humans, Adam and Eve, were to eat only plants (Genesis 1:29-30). But what about dinosaurs like the "king tyrant terrible lizard," *Tyrannosaurus Rex*? Surely, God didn't make that dinosaur a plant eater! Or did He?

Come to think of it, how can a scientist decide what an animal ate by looking at its fossil skeleton? Often, scientists compare the shape of the teeth and fossil bones to those of living reptiles. If the live animals eat meat, then the fossil animal with the same kind of skeleton and teeth is believed to have dined in the same way.

But let's examine more closely the teeth and jaws of *Tyrannosaurus Rex*. The teeth are long and sharp—they seem to be the kind of teeth that would be just right for a terrible killer. But when we look closer, we can see a problem. The teeth have shallow roots. What do you think would happen if *Tyrannosaurus* sunk his teeth into the leg of a five-ton galloping *Triceratops*? He would probably leave a few of his best teeth behind! Although those long, sharp teeth of *Tyrannosaurus* may not have been good for fighting, they would be excellent for ripping the rinds off of ripe melons.

If this seems hard to believe, on the next page is an example of a living animal with very sharp "meat eating" teeth that is not carnivorous at all. Look at the dagger-like teeth of the spider monkey. This monkey eats only fruit. What do we know for *sure* about a dinosaur fossil with long, sharp teeth? Long, sharp teeth do not always mean that an animal is, or was, a meat eater. We can believe God when He tells us that in the beginning all animals, including *Tyrannosaurus Rex*, ate plants—maybe even ripe, juicy melons!

Diets can't always be judged by the shape of teeth. This spider monkey is a fruit eater.

APPENDIX B: A Biblical Creation Model of Earth History

Historical Event	Reference
Miraculous creation of Earth, and all living organisms on earth: Every living organism was created to reproduce after its own kind; Creation was complete in six days; The ancestors of animals living today were created during the same week as humans.	Genesis 1 and 2 Exodus 20:11
A global Flood-Judgement: Flood waters covered the entire Earth destroying all land animals (and humans), except those saved on Noah's Ark; At least one pair of each kind of air-breathing animal was miraculously saved—including animal kinds representing the dinosaurs.	Genesis 6, 7, and 8 2 Peter 3:3-7 Psalm 104
Repopulation of a much changed Earth by plants and animals after the Flood: Initial dispersal of animals away from the region where the Ark landed followed by dispersal of human tribes and family groups after their common language was taken away at the Tower of Babel; The planet still suffered episodes of catastrophic upheaval as geological structures adjusted to the effects of the Flood and its miraculous removal by uplifting mountain ranges and containment in newly formed ocean basins.	Genesis 8, 9, and 11 Job 37 and 38 Psalm 104

For a complete listing of references detailing the scientific evidences and apologetic necessity of the doctrine of Biblical Creation, write the author.

Biological Evidence

No biological mechanism exists that allows one organism to change into an entirely different kind of organism —either in gradual stages or in sudden leaps.

Biological stastis (fixity of kinds) is the rule; however, an organism's genetic make-up and other factors, such as isolation and environment, can effect species development within a kind.

Present populations of humans and animals are consistent with a model starting with small reproducing groups less than 10,000 years ago.

Extinction of animal species since the Flood due to a changing environment—particularly the giant animals (megafauna). Dispersal patterns of humans and archeological remains attest to the changing post-Flood environment. Human legends and myth.

Geological Evidence

After studying millions of fossils, no legitimate intermediate forms (organisms showing characteristics of evolving into another more complex kind of organism) have been discovered.

Catastrophic (not gradual) burial of billions of dead organisms in thousands of feet of layered mud all over the earth.

Warm ocean model gives credence to a rapid and short post-Flood Age of Ice.

Relatively insignificant amounts of sediments in ocean basins.

Lack of evidence for continental drift.

Continuing earthquakes and volcanic activity.

TEACHERS

A *Teacher's Guide* for using *Dinosaurs and the Bible* in elementary grades is available from the author. Write "Teacher's Dinosaur Guide," P.O. Box 177, New Home, TX 79383 for more information.

ACKNOWLEDGEMENTS

Dinosaurs and the Bible was written to give students, parents, and teachers a closer look at these amazing reptiles God created. The story of dinosaurs continues to unfold as scientists discover and study new fossils. As knowledge grows, we find that the biblical record of Creation, the Flood, and Noah's Ark provides the better explanation of the fossil record. I am grateful to the many scientists who have contributed to ideas used in this book, although the author alone is responsible for the information and its presentation.

A special thanks needs to be given to the following people: Dr. Carl Baugh, Director of the Creation Evidences Museum, Glen Rose, Texas, whose investigations into Paluxy River sediments is providing new evidence for humans and dinosaurs co-existing in the pre-Flood world; John Rajca and Mark Dinsmore for their invaluable help in research, writing, and editing; Dr. Gary Parker, Dr. Carl Wieland, and Ken Ham for their excellent suggestions on improving the manuscript.

I would like also to acknowledge the following artists. Their contributions can never be praised too highly: Marvin Ross (Institute for Creation Research, San Diego): Cover-"The Eighth Day." Jonathan Chong (Aslan Design, Canada): "Behemoth," p.8; "melon eating dinosuar," p.43; "Flying reptiles," p.30-31; "Mokele Mbembe," p.36-37. Jay Wegter (San Diego): "Job," p.6-7; "Days of Creation," p.14-15; "Duckbilled dinosaurs," p.26-27; "Flood: Before, During, and After," p.38-39. Ron Hight (San Diego): "Mary Ann," p.10-11; "Krakatoa," p.18-19; "Comet," p.21. Doug Schmitt (San Diego): "Whale of a Tale," p.13. Steve Cardno (Creation Science Foundation, Australia): "Graveyard," p.22; "Coelacanths," p.32-33.

Photograph Credits: Creation Science Foundation, p.43; Carl Baugh, p.29; Ronald Calais, p.16; Dave Unfred, p.17; American Museum of Natural History, p.24-25, 27; Michihiko Yano, p.35.